Comments from some of Marilyn's c

"I am moved to provide the highest recommendation for Marilyn. I have had the privilege of working with Marilyn for the past few years. She has done a wonderful job of developing my personal website. My site is highly complex — involving many articles, interviews, and videos. She has done a great job of making it user friendly. I have received feedback from hundreds of people about my site. It has all been very positive! Marilyn deserves much of the credit for this success. Along with her great technical job in developing my site, Marilyn has been a pleasure to work with."

Marshall Goldsmith
Best-selling author: *What Got You Here Won't Get You There*
www.MarshallGoldsmithLibrary.com

"If you have the chance to hire Coach Marilyn, do yourself a favor and do it! I have worked with Marilyn on several large projects: the gala launch of a new organizational partnership, a hurry-up web conversion project, the rebranding of a website, and the development and organization of a partnership project. I found her technical skills to be superb; whether the question was about how to convert video, how to change a flash movie or how to track response to Google ads, Marilyn knows how.'

'But then, so do a lot of tech consultants. What makes Marilyn so special is that her technical expertise comes bundled with superb interpersonal skills. She can help you think through both the technical and the human part of the problem, then help you implement the solution. Best of all, she's a joy to have around as a colleague. She's not only happy to pitch in and get the job done, she does it with it humor and compassion."

Nicolette Toussaint, Communications Director
Alliant International University, San Francisco, California

"Since I've always considered myself a highly organized person, I was somewhat surprised and very pleased by what Ms. McLeod was able to offer me. She took ideas from a brainstorming session with about two dozen supporters and integrated that material into a coherent framework. She also made some very helpful suggestions for how I could improve my personal system of organization."

Gary Baran, Former Executive Director, CNVC

Also by Marilyn McLeod:

Conscious Networking
Finding and Creating Your Ideal Communities

Peer Coaching Reference
Extending Your Coaching Dollar

Recession or Plenty
7 Steps to Success in Business & in Life

Secrets of Self Publishing
Digital Tools for Publishing and Marketing

Social Media Series:

Social Media for Beginners
Step by Step for Small Business

Social Media for Small Business
Tips for Using Your Time Effectively

How to Work with Your Web Developer
Asking the Right Questions

Social Media Strategy
Navigating the New World Online

Social Media Workbook
Creating Your Master Plan

How to Work with Your Web Developer

ASKING THE RIGHT QUESTIONS

by Marilyn McLeod

Consider the Possibility Press
www.considerthepossibilitypress.com

How to Work with Your Web Developer
Asking the Right Questions

For information:

Consider the Possibility Press
http://www.considerthepossibilitypress.com
P O Box 703
Cardiff-by-the-Sea, CA 92007 U.S.A.
+1-760-644-2284

Library of Congress Catalog Card Number

International Standard Book Number
978-0-9822290-8-8

Printed in the United States of America

How to Work with Your Web Developer
Asking the Right Questions

This book is written for people who have a website and would like to work more effectively with their web developer.

Quickest route to something usable in this book:
Chapter 4 "Social Media - Your Role and When to Get Help" (page 43)

The social media landscape changes very quickly. Some content in this book may change by the time you read this. To keep up with changes look for future editions of this book. You may also follow me on Twitter @marilynmcleod and find the social media book series Facebook Fan Page via www.CoachMarilyn.com.

Enjoy the book and your adventures in social networking!

Join me online as we learn more together!

Marilyn McLeod
San Diego 2010

www.CoachMarilyn.com

Introduction

You're probably very busy doing what you do to bring in new customers and deliver your products and services, and you're probably working with a web developer or designer to handle the technical side of your online presence.

You may be thinking you're not 'tuned in' to social media, and you probably don't really enjoy doing this yourself, anyway.

This books helps you understand the general territory of online marketing, search engine optimization and social media from your web developer's point of view.

Does your web developer know how to do all of these things? Don't be too hard on them if they don't. The Internet is a large and complicated place, and we're all learning together. We all tend to specialize, and only learn something new when we need to. The point is … is your developer interested in learning, and if so, will you pay the price for their learning curve, or will they invest some of their own time to learn something new? Or is what you're wanting outside their area of expertise? You may need a team of Internet professionals to address what you want to accomplish online.

Throughout the book you'll find questions you can ask to give you more insight into how your developer can help you meet your online goals.

If you need more support, check my website for webinars, teleclasses and coaching opportunities. www.CoachMarilyn.com @marilynmcleod

About the Author

Marilyn McLeod has been both a consumer and a provider of Internet technology services over the past fourteen years. She's studied every phase of website development in order to communicate effectively with Internet professionals.

She began working with Internet technologies and online marketing in 1996, back in the days when Macromedia Flash 2 fit on a 3.5" disk, registering a domain name involved sending an email to netsol and paying $70/year, and a whois search displayed all the domain names registered with that character string so you could see at a glance who your competition was online.

In the 90s you couldn't say she was especially enthusiastic about the whole Internet thing, or even computers for that matter, much preferring nature to the digitized world. After spending a summer living happily in a primitive home in the north woods of Minnesota, she moved to downtown Minneapolis and took a job where she was surrounded by three computer systems. A short time later she decided to come to terms with her new digital landscape, put up a Do Not Disturb sign for a week while she poured over computer manuals, and thus she went from being afraid of computers to becoming the resident expert.

As she learned more about business, became a small business owner herself, a consultant and finally a coach to other small business owners, she brought her technology with her and applied it to her client's projects.   In 1996 when she decided to put her coaching business online, she chose to learn the technology behind the website. This turned out not to be a simple task, as she found that many discreet technologies came into play. She also discovered that experts in one technology often had no awareness of the technology that came before or after their little part of the spectrum. In this book series Marilyn shares her exploration of social media.

Table of Contents

CHAPTER 1

How a Website Works

ℰↄ

When I first began creating websites in 1996, I thought it was one technology: What I saw onscreen is what I created in html (a computer programming language with a set of code tags that web developers use to create web pages). Then I noticed there were also the images and I learned about Photoshop (a software program web developers use to create images for web pages). I tried using several html editors, settling for awhile on FrontPage, which offered several shortcuts to technology. The usefulness of the shortcuts was short lived, so I continued exploring and finally settled on Dreamweaver and HomeSite as my html editors of choice.

As I explored beyond FrontPage to get the results I wanted, I learned much about what's behind the scenes. Each time I studied a new facet of the puzzle, I found that even one facet was made up of several applications or facets of its own, and so on.

The technology continues to evolve. I started one 875-hour course in the fall to learn how web servers work. By the end of the course the software program (or set of software programs, really) we'd been studying for nine months was replaced by a new version. That's just the way it is.

How do I deal with this? If I want to identify with one technology, I keep using it regularly myself, and update my software each time there's a new version. I go through a learning curve each time the software is updated, but it's less of a learning curve than when I first learned that particular piece of software, or that technology in general. After awhile I learned to look for patterns in concepts, which makes my skills more versatile. When I approach a new piece of software it's easier for me to find my way around because I know the technology behind the interface, and I know what functions to look for in the software. I know what they're supposed to do. So my skills have become less software specific and based more on the functionality I need.

I'm writing this book from that perspective … a broad view of the way things work, rather than going into detail about each specific piece of the puzzle you'll come across. One web developer is going to have a different set of skills and a different personality from the next one, and the software you and they will be dealing with will probably change by the time this book is published. But the principles remain the same, or at least they have since 1996 when I began my journey online.

I'll talk you through the principles and you can apply them to your situation. My theory: If you understand the lay of the land, including your options, and I give you a reference point, you'll be able to navigate this world more effectively. That's my goal with this book.

What You See Onscreen

When you look at a web page, there may be several elements:

Text

Some text on the page is created by the html code (behind the scenes). You can tell which part of the page this is by trying to select it (click and drag your cursor over the text). If you can select the text, it's html text. Usually the text in the middle of the page is made from html. Another clue is it's probably not the fancy text on the page.

Look for a fancier looking bit of text and try to click and drag across that text to select it. It might change color or size, or do nothing as your cursor gets close, but you can't select it. This text is made from an image.

Images

Most graphic elements on a web page are made from a graphic. These might be photographs or words made to look fancier than the plain looking text in the main part of the web page.

Sometimes these images move. Just because they move doesn't mean they're a video. They might be animated images … a set of related images the web designer or developer has programmed to display one right after another.

Flash

Some visual elements on a page are created in Flash, which kind of looks like a cross between a moving image and a video. Flash is a multi-faceted technology which can contain almost any kind of content (text, photos, audio, video, interactive forms). You may hear the term "Flash site". This means the content of the website is written primarily in Flash code as opposed to html code. Even Flash sites are always contained within at least a basic html page.

Video

You might see a variety of video types or video players on web pages. These appear with some form of play button, and sometimes a pause button or other controls. When they stop playing smoothly and begin to sputter, or start and stop irregularly, it's usually because the download bandwidth is slower than the speed of player, so the player has to wait for the download to catch up with the playhead (the pointer that indicates where you are in terms of watching the video). When you see a line near the playhead and you see a color moving across the line and past the playhead, it usually means the download has surpassed where you are in terms of watching the video, so that usually means it won't sputter.

Audio

You might see audio in a variety of ways on a web page. You may be given a set of controls to play and pause the audio. You may be given a link to click on. Sometimes the link will either allow you to download the audio (like an mp3) to your own computer so you can listen to it later, or you can listen to it from the website where you found it.

If you right click on the link, it may say 'Save Target As' or something like that. If so, navigate to where you want to save the mp3 on your computer and save it. If you just click on the link, it'll probably open up a new window with some player controls.

How Web Pages Work

If you've decided to use a blog instead of a website, working through this section may not be as relevant to you. Glance through the material anyway because it'll help you understand later sections of this book. Pay special attention whenever you see the words 'keyword' or 'search phrase'.

Static and Dynamic Websites

In 1996 most websites contained one-way communication. The website owner would ask the web developer to upload some text and images to their website, and that's the way it would stay until the website owner decided to change something. Many websites are still like this. They are called 'static websites' or 'brochure-ware'. There's nothing wrong with this. It's just a matter of whether or not that type of website provides you and your target audience with what you need.

Dynamic websites contain interactive elements that allow a website visitor to interact with the website. This would include contact forms and pages where the visitor types information or makes choices of some kind and then clicks a submit button, which then may display the results of the selected information on the screen for the website visitor to see.

Dynamic websites are wonderful, and they are what has revolutionized the Internet. They're what allow you to look up your current bank accounts, post to a blog, get driving directions, order a book, or send status updates on social media sites. They are also a source of vulnerability, because if they allow you to interact with their website, then hackers who have less benign intentions also have access. There are several ways behind the scenes and on the web page to add security, such as those funny looking letters and numbers you're sometimes asked to type in before you can click the submit button (called a captcha). Sometimes they keep the bad guys out, and sometimes the most well-protected sites have trouble. I don't have any solutions; I'm not a security expert. I'm just giving you the lay of the land so you can make your own choices.

HTML

Following is a sample of html code. This is the basic 'container' for each web page content, regardless of what the web page displays or how it was created. I'll go through each element below. It's actually pretty logical and simple to understand. Most html elements have a beginning and ending part of the tag, and the stuff in between is what displays on the web page. Look for these elements in the following example of html:

html
head
title
meta
body
img
a

Example of HTML:

```
<html>
<head>
<title>Coach Marilyn</title>
<meta name="keywords" content="this is a list of my keywords,
and key phrases, separated, by commas" />
<meta name="description" content="This is the 25 word
description of the website." />
</head>
<body>
This section between 'body tags' is the visible part of the web page.
<img src="image-name.gif" width="150" height="10" border="0"
alt="This is a description of the image." />
<a href="http://www.CoachMarilyn.com" target="_blank"> This is
a clickable link.</a>
</body>
</html>
```

Sometimes you'll see them capitalized, such as <HTML> instead of
<html>. It doesn't matter; the tags work the same whether they're
capitalized or not.

Here's what they do:

html

Every web page starts with a beginning <html> tag and ends
with an ending </html> tag. If you find a web page that displays
without an ending </html> tag, the web developer was lucky.
Sometimes the browsers (Internet Explorer, Firefox, Chrome,
Safari, Opera, etc.) make up for incomplete code and display the
page anyway.

head

Items in the <head> tag don't show up on the web page visually. They have various jobs to do. You might find a link to a style sheet, which defines the type of font, the color of links, whether links are underlined or not ... that sort of thing. You will hopefully find title and meta tags in the head tag because they're important to search engines.

title

The words between <title> and </title> are the words that appear at the very top line of your browser window. Check it out on your own website. If it says "Untitled" it means your web developer didn't add a title tag.

Whatever is in the title tag is also what appears as the first line in the search engine results. Try it out! Go to a search engine and type in your website. Look at the search results. If your web page says "Untitled" at the top of the browser window, your listing on the search engine will also begin with "Untitled".

meta

There are various types of meta tags which communicate with search engines. The two you're most interested in for search engine ranking are the meta description tag and meta keyword tag. The keyword tag is what the search engines use to help categorize your web page, and the description tag is the text that appears as the description in search engine results. If you don't have a description tag, the search engine may just display the first few lines of text they find on your web page.

body

Whatever is contained between body tags is what can be displayed visually on your web page when you look there in a browser. If the html code is not well formed (meaning the ending part of a tag is missing or misspelled, or they're out of order), there may be parts of your web page content that are not displaying.

It can be tricky for a web developer to create clean, well-formed code. This is especially true for dynamic websites, where a missing semicolon or an extra \ can make all the difference between whether a web page works or doesn't work. It can take a web developer literally hours to find the offending section of code, which is called debugging the code. It's easier to debug static websites, because there are software programs like Dreamweaver that often highlight the problem and make it easier for the developer to identify and fix. In addition, there are fewer moving parts and variables in a static website.

img

Any image you see appearing on your website requires two parts: the actual image (which either has been created or optimized in a software program like Photoshop), and the link which tells the html where to find the actual image, and how to display the image.

<img src="image-name.gif" width="150" height="10" border="0" alt="This is a description of the image." />

In the code above <img starts the image tag, and /> ends the image tag. The part that says image-name.gif is the actual image with the name given to it when it was saved. The image file has to be saved in the exact place on the server that shows up in the image tag, or instead of seeing the image you'll see that weird little icon thing you don't know what to do with. The browser didn't know what to do with it either, and put that weird little thing there to tell you there's supposed to be an image, but the browser can't find it. That's called a 'broken link'.

The width and height part of the image tag may or may not be there. If the image looks distorted on screen, it probably means the width and height of the actual image doesn't match the width and height the image tag tells the browser to expect. If the tag can be edited to match the actual image, it's usually an easy fix.

The border tag tells the browser whether or not to put a line around the image, and if so, how wide the border should be. It's sometimes nice to put a black border of "1" around a photo; it just makes it look cleaner. Sometimes that creates a black line around an image that doesn't fit with the effect the image is trying to create, so then it's a good idea to have a border of "0".

By the way, each browser (Internet Explorer, Firefox, Chrome, Safari, Opera, etc.) renders html code a bit differently, so a developer has to design for a middle of the road solution that will work acceptably in all browsers.

Sometimes an image is used as a button to create a clickable link. In this case the browser usually puts a border around the image. If this doesn't look right, just set the border to "0".

The "alt" part of the image tag is important to search engines and screen readers. When you look at a web page you'll see the image visually and you'll know it says "Click Here" but screen readers and search engines only see image-name.gif. The information contained in the alt tag interprets the meaning of image-name.

gif into something with more information they can use. You can usually read the alt tag by rolling your cursor over an image without clicking on the image.

Optimizing an image means bringing it into a software program like Photoshop and exporting it with settings that reduce the file size without degrading the visual clarity of the image.

a

Another important tag, the anchor tag creates links. It might link to another web page, or it might link to a named anchor on the same web page.

<a href="http://www.CoachMarilyn.com" target="_blank"> This is a clickable link.</a>

This is a link to an outside web page. The target part of the tag tells the browser whether to open a new browser window to display CoachMarilyn.com, or whether to overwrite the current window. _blank tells it to open in a new window. This is a good idea when you don't want to send the visitor completely away from the web page they're currently on; you just want to help them find other information temporarily, so when they close the new window you've sent them to, your web page still appears beneaath that new window.

Here's how it works when you have a long page and you want to send the visitor down to the appropriate section of the current page. This is called a 'named anchor'.

<a href="#schedule">

This would send the visitor to the matching named anchor tag elsewhere on the page:

<a name="schedule">

Both, of course, would have an ending </a> tag with clickable words in between the beginning and ending parts of the tag.

Find HTML on Your Own Website

How can you find these hidden tags on your own website? While you're looking at your web page in a browser (Internet Explorer, Firefox, Chrome, Safari, Opera etc.) right click on a part of the page that looks like it doesn't have any text or images on it. You should get a dialog box with an option to View Source or something like that. Click on View Source and see what you get!

It'll look much more complicated than the html code examples above, but you'll find these same basic elements in your own web page code.

How Websites Work

Well, I'm not going to bore you with the details of how web servers work. I do think it is important to understand the basics of how web pages communicate with other parts of the puzzle to do their work.

Your Domain Name

Remember back when you claimed your domain name? You went to a domain name registrar (like GoDaddy, Network Solutions, etc.), found one you liked that was available, and paid some money. You actually didn't buy it; you just claimed the right to use it for the specific number of years you paid for, and if you don't renew and let it lapse, someone else can gain control of the domain name. You'll still have your website, but no one will be able to get to it using your domain name. In fact, if someone else registers it and creates their own website, when your customers type in your domain name to find you, they'll find the new owner's website instead.

Ways to help you keep your domain name:

- Make sure you are listed as the owner or registrant. This gives you the most control of any role. The owner can change the password and delete administrators. If you're not listed as the owner, then whoever is listed can forget to renew, can refuse to give you access, can redirect the domain name somewhere besides your website, etc.

- Make sure you keep your email address current in your domain name record. If you're planning to change your email address, keep your old one for a month or two while you begin using your new one. Use this time to update your email address in your domain name record, so your domain name registrar can find you at either email address while they're updating their records to your new email.

- Make sure you remember your password, especially if you've decided to use a proxy account for privacy reasons. If you can't remember your password, you may not be able to retrieve it from the proxy (who you hired to protect you from prying eyes or people who might try to steal your account from you, which means they'll be suspicious of you trying to break in as well), so you might not be able to log in to renew or maintain your account, and may eventually lose your domain name.

Your Website Files

Your web developer created a series of html files, image files and other files which make up the content of your website. These are actual computer documents that can be copied onto a disk or uploaded to a web hosting account on a web server. You paid your web developer a lot of money one time to create these files for you, and less money throughout the year when you want updates.

Your Web Server

You're probably paying by the month or by the year for your web hosting account. Don't use the free versions if you want to appear professional. Your web hosting company has a room full of computers specifically configured to hold web pages like yours, and to make them easily accessible to people browsing on the Internet.

If you have a large, busy website you may have a dedicated server, where the entire computer contains only your files. More likely you've ordered an account on a shared server, where you're one of up to hundreds of accounts with a little piece of the pie. If you're on a shared server and you notice your website is slow or doesn't work sometimes, it could be that the web developer didn't optimize your images properly or there is something wrong with their code, or it could just be someone else you're sharing the server with got really busy and took all the bandwidth. If this is an intermittent problem, it's probably the web server. See if you can move to a server with more bandwidth, which will probably cost more money.

When you set up your web hosting account, your web hosting company assigned you an account name. As a company they maintain a separate server that keeps track of all the account names and what domain names are associated with them, which is called their name server. In order for people who type your domain name into their browsers to actually see your web page, the correct names of your hosting company's name servers have to match what's listed in your domain name record (with your domain name registrar) as your name servers for that domain name. Your domain name registrar will ask for at least two name servers (which you obtain from your web hosting company).

Let's Watch It Work

Okay, now you have all the pieces: domain name, website files, and server.

Let's go back to your web page. You open up your browser of choice (Internet Explorer, Firefox, Chrome, Safari, Opera etc.) and type in your domain name. Up pops your web page, just as you ordered! How did that happen?

You typed in your domain name. The name server in the sky looked this up and found the name of your domain name registrar, and asked them where your web pages are stored.

Your domain name registrar pointed them to your web hosting company's name server, which in turn referred your browser to the space on the particular computer in their computer room where your web developer uploaded your website files. And there was a match!! Or not. If you get a 'page not found' then there wasn't a match. For now let's say there was a match.

Your web server sent back the content of the html pages and image files to your browser, which your browser sent to your computer that you're using to view the web page, and your computer saved the html pages and image files (that your web developer created and uploaded onto your web server) in a temporary folder on your computer. That's called 'caching' your website files. Then the browser displays the results for you to see.

Next time you go to this web page, your browser may go to these cached files instead of going to all of the trouble of the long trip to your web server. Or sometimes your Internet Service Provider caches the web pages on their server for awhile to save bandwidth and cost, which is sometimes why, when your web developer says they've made a change to your web page but you don't see the change … you're probably looking at the old cached version. How to remedy this: If you're using an AOL browser, open up Internet Explorer, Firefox or one of the other browsers and try that one to view the new page.

If you still don't see the new version, try clicking the reload button, or hold Shift while you're clicking the reload button, usually at the top of your browser window. This forces the browser to make the long trip back to your web server to see what's there. If none of this works, ask your web developer if they really did upload the right file. Sometimes they uploaded the one next to it on their computer! Or try a new browser program on your computer that you haven't used in awhile, so any cached versions of the web page for that browser have timed out of that browser's cache history.

Let's say there wasn't a match when your browser got to the server, so the server sent the 'page not found' message back to you through your browser. What happened there?

- It could be that you typed an incorrect character, or if you clicked on a link to get there, perhaps there was a misspelling in the anchor tag which contained the link. Pay particular attention to the portion of the url after the .com/ or .org/ etc. This part of the url may be case sensitive.

- It could be that your web server is experiencing problems. Call technical service at your web hosting company and ask if there's an issue. They may either say they're aware of it and working on it, or thank you for letting them know, or say everything is working fine from their side.

- It could be that somehow the web page was deleted from your server, or the spelling of the file name has changed since the link was created. Ask whoever updates your website to check it out.

- It could be your domain name has expired, in which case it's time to call your domain name registrar and see how you can remedy the situation.

If the web page your browser requested from the server contained an interactive form, then there is a second layer of functionality when you interact with that page. The submit button on the web page actually calls a server script which your web developer creates. They will choose the scripting language they're most comfortable with, and that works on the type of software your web server uses.

Microsoft servers often use ASP, Cold Fusion and sometimes PHP. Apache servers use PHP, PERL, and other open source scripting languages.

What is open source? There are basically two flavors of web server systems. One is provided by Microsoft, which carries a hefty price tag for people who want to use their products, and is supported by Microsoft staff. The source code is protected from access. The other is open source, which includes Linux, Apache, MySQL, PHP, PERL and others.

The open source part means in most cases there is no cost to use the software, and the software is supported by a community of volunteer developers who update the code and answer questions posted by other developers working with the software. Any developer can make updates to the source code, as long as they freely share their updates with the community. The principal developers test updates thoroughly before releasing a new version of Apache.

After you click the submit button, your browser sends the information you've just typed into the form back from your browser to the web server, which goes into its database tables and either looks up what you asked for or updates the tables with the information you provided, then sends back a message from the database (through the usual channels) to your browser, where your browser displays the results for you to see. The results are not cached, which is why you can't use the browser's back button with those pages.

Summary

- When using computer and Internet technology, be flexible. Links, accustomed buttons and navigation may change. Learn how things work so you can find alternatives as interfaces and technologies evolve.

- A website is made up of what you see onscreen as a visitor, and also what's behind the scenes talking to search engines, the server and database.

- Domain name, website files and the server interact with each other to display what you see in your browser when you go to your website.

CHAPTER 2

How Search Engines Work

℘

You've got your wonderful website working now. How do you get the attention of search engines?

Search Engine Optimization

First let's look at what your website is set up to communicate to search engines when they arrive at your site.

Search engines care about satisfying their customers. Their customers are the people doing searches. People doing searches want to find content relevant to the words they typed into the search engine. This means search engines care about the content of your website being relevant to the search terms they're using to categorize your website in their database.

This means it's important for you to give the search engines a clear message about each page you want them to index in their database.

The first part of this takes the most time: Find the most relevant search terms for your content. You can do this quickly, or you can go into depth and stay on top of current trends, taking a lot of time. It really depends on how much time and money you have, and how important staying on top of those nuances matters to what you want to accomplish with your website.

If basically you have a static website that you want to use as credibility and to give customers and potential customers information to help them do business with you, and you're not looking to make a big splash online but simply use your website to support what you're already doing offline, maybe it's not a big deal.

I'll just take you through the basics. Going into depth is another whole book. You can stop at any stage and you'll have the benefit of your research to that point. It's an unending project, so don't feel bad when you get to the point of saying 'enough'!

First think of keywords you'd use in a search engine if you were looking for someone like you. Go to a search engine and type them in. Do you find sites similar to what you do? If not, keep trying new search terms until you find some good ones that match. Write the good ones down.

You can also put them into Wordtracker's keyword suggestion tool to get other versions: http://freekeywords.wordtracker.com

Create a new Word or text document and begin keeping track of the relevant search terms you find. Save it in the RESOURCES folder (see Volume 1 *Social Media for Beginners*) on your computer under Keywords.

Next I'll teach you how to do some detective work.

Go the search engine again, and type in one of the search terms you thought was especially effective. You'll get a list of search results. Chances are the page of results will look this way:

- A few selected listings at the top, perhaps with a slight background color
- A list of brief links on the right
- A long list of results in the middle of the page

- Perhaps another list lower on the page with links to video and audio

What does this mean?

The few selected listings at the top, and the list of brief links on the right, are probably paid listings. The website owners chose the search term you just typed in, and they placed a competitive bid, which means they agreed to pay the search engine however much money they bid for that search term whenever someone (like you) clicks on their sponsored (or paid) link. Though search engines have made other refinements to their policies these days, basically whoever has the highest bid gets the top listing on the page, and so on.

The long list of results you see in the middle of the page … those listings are earned. The website owners or web developers worked with the content of the page to make it search engine friendly. Another way of saying this is they optimized the web page for search engines … search engine optimization, or SEO.

Basically they chose a search phrase or two and worked with the portions of the website the search engine will see (html text, image alt tags, meta keyword and description tags, for instance) so the search engine sees relevance within the page for those search phrases. Hopefully when a search engine comes along it'll agree the web page is about whatever the meta keyword tag says it's about, and index it along with those search phrases in their database. Then hopefully when one of your potential customers is looking for someone like you, they type in your search phrase, and your web page is listed in their search results.

But where is it listed? Probably not as the first listing, unless you've chosen some exotic new phrase and your potential customer knows exactly what to type in.

Search engines have been around for awhile and chances are you have some competition from other websites for your search terms. Your website may be listed in the results, but it might be on page 250, or 1,000,250. When you're doing a search, how often do you go beyond the first few pages, or even the first or second listing on the first page?

How do you get listed on the first page?

Whether or not that's even possible has something to do with the search phrases you're choosing. If your search phrase yields millions of results when you do the search, you've got lots of competition for that search phrase. Can you make it more specific? For instance, if I use the search phrase 'coach' I'll not only get people looking for a person to help them with some issue, I'll also get people who are looking for Coach handbags, or a Coach bus. How do I make this more efficient for both me and the person searching for what I do? By being more specific.

There are many varieties of coaches these days. The last time I checked, the search term 'executive coach' was expensive … at least $25-$50 per click just to get close to the top listings in paid search. That means there's lots of competition from executive coaching companies with deep pockets. If I'm an individual coach I probably won't want to compete head to head on that turf.

One trick is to keep getting more specific in your search terms until you filter out all the people who aren't part of your target audience, and until you describe exactly what you do for the people who know exactly what they're looking for. That's called 'long tail search phrases'. In your meta keyword tag you'd put the whole phrase between commas, and probably use most of the same words as well individually, with commas between each word, so the search engines would know you're about executives and coaching for instance, but also about executive coaching.

For example:

<meta name="keywords" content="executive coach, executive coaching, executive, coach, coaching, coching">

Do people easily misspell whatever it is you do? Adding misspellings to your meta keyword tag is a great way to help those people find you in a much shorter list of search results.

Back to your search results page using your best search phrase. How did the people in the middle of the page get listed on the first page? Well, let's look first at the keywords they used in their meta tags.

Click on the link in the search results for the first website listed. Remember ... you're clicking on the first website in the middle section, not at the very top (if there are sponsored links at the top) or the sponsored listings on the right. You want to look at websites that have earned their way to that page.

Now you're looking at the web page as a web visitor would view it. How does it look? Is there a lot of text? What is the page about as you look visually? What's in the title tag at the top of the browser window?

Remember how I showed you to View Source earlier? This will help you now as you find out what other websites like yours are doing with their search terms. Find an area of the page that looks like there's nothing there ... no images or text ... and right click. Choose View Source or similar. Now you're looking at the jibberish (html) I showed you on your own website.

Do you see the html tag? How about the head tag? Beneath the head tag you'll find the meta tags. Is there a meta description tag? A meta keyword tag?

Record Your Research

Create a new Word or text document and do this:

Click back on the actual web page. Copy and paste the url at the top of the page (the domain name etc.) into your Word document. Now click back on the page source. Copy and paste the two meta tags and title tag into your Word document under the url. If you want to be thorough, create a new folder in your RESOURCES directory on your computer called Keyword Research and save the Word document there. Then go to the page source with jibberish and File, Save As using the name of the website (either domain name or from the title tag) or the search phrase you used to find the website. You can now close that file source jibberish page.

Go back to your search results, and do the same thing with the second listing on the page. If you saved the first source file with the search phrase, add a '2' after the search phrase in the file name. The next time add a '3', etc. Do this for at least three listings on the search results page. Then do the same thing for each search phrase you thought might be useful.

No Meta Tags

So what did you find? You may have found something interesting … some websites at the top of the search results list may have had no meta tags at all! How did that happen?!

There are other factors the search engines weigh when they're ranking websites. What exactly do they factor into their calculations and how much weight is given to each variable? Well, the search engines were changing their algorithms monthly when I began working with them in 1996, and every year they've gotten better at creating barriers to web developers gaming their systems. Remember, search engines want to serve up relevant results to their customers. I'm not suggesting you use what I'm telling you to game the system. Don't do things like listing your keywords hundreds of times in the same color as the background. It won't work, anyway … the search engines were wise to that in 1996. I'd like you to use this information to help you fashion a legitimate website that provides quality content on your topic to people who want to read quality content about your topic.

So it's a guessing game in terms of improving your search ranking. I'm just giving you a list of factors that I've seen search engines use over the years, the principles of which will probably last indefinitely.

Back to the websites listed on the first page with no meta tags. What happened there?

Chances are those websites had lots of incoming links. This means the search engines saw a large number of other legitimate, quality websites linking to that particular web page. The more website visitors the website receives, the more 'points' it gets in terms of being a quality website. The content of these other websites probably matched the content of the website listed, improving their relevancy score. Another way their relevancy score for those search terms may have been improved is the words in the link from those other websites probably contained the search terms you used to find their website.

Following the Trail

How can you check this out? Go back to your search engine and try searching on this:

Link: http://put the actual url of the page you found here

You'll get a listing of websites linking into the url you typed in. I've noticed this doesn't always include all of the websites linking in, but it gives you a good idea of what's going on. If you change the url slightly, such as adding http:// or removing it so you just use www, you'll get different results. Try typing in just the domain name without everything after the .com/, .org, etc..

Click on some of the pages that came up in the search results. See if you can find the link going to the web page you found initially. You may find something interesting again ... sometimes these incoming links are contained within the website they're going to. I've noticed the search engines seem to give these 'incoming' links the same weight they give incoming links from other websites.

Optimizing Your Website

Because of the importance of internal 'incoming' links, it might be a good idea to consider your search terms when you choose words for your website navigation. Use text links with these search terms within your website to point to the main page (or landing page) about that particular topic, so the content of that landing page is very relevant to the search terms linking to the page.

Some places on your web page to add these key search phrases so search engines understand more clearly what your page is about:

- Title tag
- Meta keyword tag
- Meta description tag
- Text you read in the main part of the page, visible to website visitors
- Image alt tags
- Header tags

About header tags: when header tags like h1, h2, h3 etc. are applied to your html text, by default that text appears larger on the page than your other text, with h1 being the largest. This size visually can be changed using a stylesheet. What's important to know for now is that search engines figure your h1 tag has words describing the main topic of the page, with h2 having secondary importance, etc.

It is possible to overdo the SEO part of your website and forget the main purpose of the page: to convey relevant, quality information to people who are interested in this information. Look it over again from a web visitor's point of view. Is it easy to find the relevant information? Is it easy to read, or has the process of adding search terms to the readable content rendered it weird or unreadable? Does it contain information that's useful and timely? You really have two audiences here: the search engines and the humans reading your website. Put yourself in your human audience's shoes and make adjustments as needed so the visual part looks right to a human.

Submit Your Website to Search Engines

It's always a good idea to list your website with the search engines. It's definitely best to do this manually rather than use some submission software that promises to get you placed on hundreds or thousands of sites. Have a 25-word description of your website, your page title, and key search words and phrases ready. Then go to each search engine individually, find their way of receiving submissions, and follow their process.

Major Search Engines:

> Ask
> Bing
> Google
> Yahoo

Others to Consider:

> AllTheWeb.com
> AltaVista
> AOL Search
> Gigablast
> HotBot
> Live
> LookSmart
> Lycos
> Netscape
> Open Directory (dmoz.org)

It might be easiest to go to one of the major search engines and search for: list website with (and then the name of the search engine) to find their current submission page.

Summary

- It's important to give search engines a clear message about each page you want them to index in their database.

- View Source to see your website from the search engine's point of view.

- Relevancy between content, keywords, search terms, and incoming links play a large part in how search engines rank your site in their search results.

- Submit your site manually to each major search engine individually.

CHAPTER 3

Designer or Developer

ℰℴ

If you're not involved directly in the technology of website development, you probably see the whole thing as I did initially: one big mass of something I didn't understand. I needed help doing even the smallest thing, and everything computer and Internet looked about the same to me. I assumed anyone who had some knowledge of any part of the computer or Internet world also had knowledge and ability in every other part of the computer and Internet world, probably because I had none.

You may have guessed by the previous paragraph that there are different sets of skills involved in computers and Internet technology. I'm here to tell you that's even a gross understatement. As long as I've been working in both worlds (computers are one thing and Internet technology is definitely another), and as long as I've been expanding my knowledge in both worlds for over 14 years now, I'm still amazed, and yes, sometimes even overwhelmed when I look at all the skill and knowledge I wish I had right now, to carry out the full extent of the projects I'd love to create online. There's always more to learn, even within the very same narrow field of even one specific niche.

So we all start where we are. And we all feel about the same way … we enjoy working with the technology we understand, and we love the feeling of satisfaction when whatever we do works out. We're all frustrated with how long it takes to figure out how to get the darned technology to do that simple thing we know it can do, and if we stick with the puzzle long enough that we finally figure it out, we realize how simple it was in the end after all ... most of the time. Sometimes it really is just that complicated.

So how can you, who is not involved behind the scenes of Internet technology, navigate your way through to get done what you want done? You'll need to know who to ask for help with a particular part of your Internet puzzle. You'll need to know what questions to ask, and key phrases that will help your Internet professional understand what it is you want done.

This chapter is about what skills various Internet professionals possess, and the next chapter is about how to ask the right questions.

There isn't a great deal of consistency in terms of how Internet professionals label themselves as it relates to the skills they possess, but I can give you some information so you can more easily identify this as you meet them and move through the process.

First, I know you're busy and you want someone else to take care of all this, but I suggest that as much of this that you understand and maintain control of (being listed as the owner of your domain name, having control of your web account, having a CD with your website files on it for instance), the more likely you are to have success over the long term as unforeseen things happen (such as the Internet professional you trusted with everything suddenly moves and forgets to tell you, or their computer crashes and they didn't back anything up ... well, you get the idea).

So I suggest the first most important person on your Internet team is **You**, even if you don't know a thing about Internet technology and you don't want to, either.

Next most important could be a **Social Media Specialist or Strategist** who can help you interpret your business and online goals into a plan you can implement, and coach you through how to get the most from your social media efforts. This is a new field, and there seem to be more social media 'experts' than there are people who want to help you follow through with the day to day work. Some Virtual Assistants are becoming knowledgeable and able to provide this kind of support. Another option is to find a social media coach who can train you and your staff at the same time, to get you and your organization started.

Some Virtual Assistants have some ability to upload or change content on a website, or to create something graphic in Photoshop, but first look at the quality of their work before agreeing to pay them for something outside of their Virtual Assistant job description. I've had the experience of one Assistant showing me the end product of a design she said she created and I was very impressed with the high quality of the design. However, the designs she created for me looked like a kindergartner was involved and had no relationship with the printed brochure she claimed she'd designed. Get a little more evidence of their skill level before making any firm agreements or committing any large sums of money.

After that … we're getting into the technical side of the Internet.

The next technical person I suggest you put on your team is a **Graphic Designer.** Anything you create, from a Twitter background to the header on your blog to a badge on your Facebook account or page on your website, will look better if someone with artistic skills in addition to the ability to use Photoshop contributes their skills.

As with Virtual Assistants, although some graphic designers know how to upload a web page or make changes, or even create html or Flash websites, don't expect them to understand very much about the underlying code. I've only known two people who really understood both the design and programming sides of a website, and they are very rare and talented people.

Speaking of **Flash**, creating a Flash movie or Flash website is a skillset unto itself. Flash is a very rich programming and design environment, and you almost have to find the Flash professional with the particular Flash skills you need. Some choices would be:

Flash Design - They are good graphic designers and know how to implement their designs in Flash, but they probably don't know how to integrate video or create interactive forms in Flash. Think of them as graphic designers with design knowledge of Flash. If your Flash movie contains large files like photos or video, ask them if they've ever created a pre-loader (which is how you can avoid the sputtering experience of playback on the Internet).

Flash Video – They understand how to edit and optimize video, and prepare an .flv file. They know how to work with a Flash Media Server to stream the video, are familiar with how to use Flash Video Components to create the .swf file that goes in the html of your web page. They'll know you need a specialized server (and they can help you sign up for a hosted account starting at about $50/month depending on your web traffic, how many web visitors will be accessing your videos simultaneously, and the file size and length of your videos) in addition to the web server you already have for your website. If your video is less than a minute long and it's a small size onscreen, you may be able to get by with a progressive download (instead of streaming) use a .swf instead of going to an .flv and Flash Media Server. In that case your .swf file would go on your server where your images also reside.

Flash Developer – They know ActionScript 2.0 or 3.0 (the scripting language Flash uses behind the scenes), as well as either Microsoft servers and ASP or Apache servers and PHP, and have experience writing programming code that interacts with a database. Ask them to demonstrate Flash interfaces they've created in the past, and look for submit buttons, scroll bars, and form elements you'd normally see on an html web page. See how long it takes for the new information to display onscreen once you click the submit button.

When you want to create visitor interactivity you'll need a **Computer Programmer** or **Website Developer** who understands how to write interactive scripts in PHP, ASP, PERL or something similar that matches your kind of web server. They hopefully also understand something about working with database tables on your Microsoft or Apache server. Ask them to demonstrate a website application they've created, and ask them to take you behind the scenes to the administrative interface if possible.

Javascript and CSS are also important to the functionality and layout of a website, but they don't interact on the server with the database. AJAX is a blend of those technoloies that may or may not access the database, but provides cool text effects without having to reload the whole web page. You'll need a Web Developer or Computer Programmer for Javascript. A Designer may be able to handle CSS. Ask them what they've done with CSS in the past.

If you're planning to have a lot of traffic accessing your website you may want to find a **System Administrator** (or sysadmin) to make sure your web server is tuned to handle the traffic and that you have enough bandwidth available for spikes in traffic. If this website includes interactive forms, you may also want to find a **Database Engineer** who can work with the person writing your interactive scripts (Website Developer or Computer Programmer) to normalize the database tables for speed and efficiency. The Database Engineer would create the database tables, and the Computer Programmer would refer to those tables in their PHP scripts, for instance. It's also important to be sure your Computer Programmer's scripts are written for efficiency, so the results come back quickly to your screen when you hit the submit button. Test this initially when website traffic is minimal or average.

Working With a Computer Programmer or Web Developer

I find very few Computer Programmers who are willing to try and figure out how another Computer Programmer wrote the code in their script. For instance, if you have ten PHP programmers, they may each be using PHP functions to accomplish the same task, but they will each have their own particular way of going about getting the job done. What this means to you is once you engage one Computer Programmer to write a script, or a set of scripts for you, if you don't like the result, you probably won't be able to find another Computer Programmer to adjust the scripts to your liking.

If you do find someone willing to make these adjustments, it will probably take them a long time to look through the code to find the places to edit, and when they make the edits it's very possible their edits will break the code somewhere else in the script, meaning they'll be spending lots of time trying to edit and fix and debug a script that's written with logic they're not very familiar with, and in the end the script may not work or it still may not do what you want it to do.

If you ask one Computer Programmer to adjust another Computer Programmer's scripts, get an agreement between the two of you that you'll only invest a certain number of hours or dollars into the project to see if it'll work. If you have problems when your time and money run out, stop and cut your losses. Often it'll just be easier to start from scratch with a new Computer Programmer. And these scripts are expensive. It's just the way it is.

One possible strategy to improve the possibility that one Computer Programmer can follow another Computer Programmer's logic is to ask the first Computer Programmer to 'comment their code'. This is kind of a lost art, as most programmers just want to focus on getting the job done and don't want to take the time to document what they're doing. It takes more time to keep making adjustments to the pseudo-code and comments as well as the working part of the code, so if you're paying by the hour, you'll be paying more – up front – for the programmer who's commenting their code. But you'll pay far less down the road when you ask them to make an edit, because even if they don't remember what your script did, they'll remember the logic they used when they wrote your script when they see their own comments throughout the code. If you find a programmer who's comfortable commenting their code, you're lucky!

Something else that's helpful to know about working with a Computer Programmer ... some things that you think would be very easy to accomplish can be very time consuming and circuitous for a programmer to carry out based on how the functionality of their scripting language and the constraints posed by the variety of technologies involved peripherally to their scripts to make them work. And some things you think might be difficult can be accomplished in only a few lines of code and be very easy for the Developer to carry out.

How do I handle this? Before I begin talking with my Web Developer, I get as clear as I can get about exactly what functionality I want and why. I think about what parts of the functionality I'm describing are non-negotiable and why. Then I schedule time with my Web Developer to talk it over.   When we meet, I tell my Web Developer what I want to accomplish (not the details of how yet), and we talk it over. He writes down my specifications as he understands them as we talk, and repeats each one back to me to make sure he understands what I want.

We start talking about how to get it done, how the interface would look for me as the administrator, and how it would look for the website visitor. He asks about my budget.   He asks where I might see this going in the future as things evolve. Then he thinks for a little while.

Now it's his turn. Based on my budget and what I want to do, maybe I could tweak my specifications this way or that in order to shorten his development time, or maybe we could add some functionality that would make the script more usable or flexible in the future as my business ideas evolve. We discuss the pros and cons for awhile, and finally settle on revised specs, and we agree on the money. It's very important for me to be clear on exactly what I expect of my web developer, and exactly when I need what completed. It's very important to him to know when he'll receive what money for doing this, and also that I'll be very available to him while he's writing the code, so he can show me incrementally what he's accomplished and I can give him feedback about whether he's going in the right direction or not before he gets too far into the project.

Another point to get clear with your developer is: Who owns the code they're writing for you? You may think because they're writing this to your specifications, that you may have the right to get a copy of the source code, and some programmers will hand it over to you. It's more likely you'll have to pay extra to get a copy of the source code, sometimes a lot more. This is because they're probably not starting from scratch writing your application or script; they're probably drawing from their own personal library of functions they've spent years and years writing and honing to perfection, and building upon these tools for your application. If you've hired a new computer programmer who's just graduated or learned the skill, this may not be as much the case. And it may take them longer to write the application with less functionality, or it may not run as quickly, or have as much ability to withstand the stress of a busy website.

It is reasonable to ask how to get a backup copy of your data from the database tables. It will probably cost more to have your developer add this functionality to your administrative console, but it's probably worth the investment to have a copy of your data. Or your developer can provide an .sql or .csv file to you regularly on a disk.

If you're given a copy of your data in a file that ends in .sql or .csv you probably won't know how to open it and use the information. Unless the file is very large, you can probably open it in Excel, and using [Data, Text to Columns] to put it into the Excel format. You can Save As an Excel spreadsheet.

Summary

- Everyone at every level of Internet expertise has basically the same experience – productivity and pleasure when working in known areas, and frustration and unproductiveness when learning something new.

- There isn't a great deal of consistency in terms of how Internet professionals label themselves.

- Clarity in agreements is important in your working relationship with Internet professionals.

CHAPTER 4

Social Media – Your Role and When to Get Help

ઠૐ

You've now learned much about websites and search engines in general. How does this translate to the new world of social media? It's actually the foundation upon which social media was built, so social media just extends it all … on steroids, actually!

The main part of the previous sections you'll carry with you into your social media world is the keyword research you did in Volume 1 of this series *Social Media for Beginners*. Keep the list close by as you're giving your Facebook Fan Page a title, adding tags to your blog posts, and writing tweets. More about that in Volume 4 of this series: *Social Media Strategy*.

Blog

Most of the search engine optimization features I described in the previous chapter are probably already built into the blog software you'll be using.

When you create a blog, you and your web developer have some choices. The main choices are whether to create a blog account on a website that's already up and running, that provides blog accounts through their software on their server, or to add blog software to your own server.

Adding blog software to your own server gives you much more flexibility in terms of customizing the look and functionality of your blog. It also increases the cost. The blog software is probably a free open source download, but your web developer has to download and configure code, continue to add updates as they're made available by the people who wrote the blog software, and deal with any security breaches that may occur.

What you can do:

- Choose a point of view for your blog (see Volume 4 of this series *Social Media Strategy*).

- Decide whether to create a blog account on an existing website, or to have your developer install blog software on your web server.

- Create an account (if available) on your blog software of choice.

- Produce quality blog posts and publish regularly, at least once a week, or even better: once a day.

- Choose one topic per blog post and sprinkle the relevant keywords and search terms through the post … not gratuitously, but in context within the article.

- Know the url to your online home base (so you can include this link in your blog post)

- Make sure your post is readable by human beings, and that it's interesting and the content is relevant and current.

- If your blog software permits, create a list of categories, and assign a category to each post.

- If your blog software permits, add the appropriate tags (relevant search terms and categories, plus important words within the post) to your post.

How your designer can help:

- Create a custom image to use as the header for your blog.

How your developer can help:

- Help you find your RSS feed url so you can add your feed to social media tools of your choice.

- Help you add any plugins or added functionality of your choice that your blog software offers.

- If you decide to host your blog on your own web space your developer can:

  - Choose a blog software package based on your web server configuration.

  - Download, install and configure software.

  - Take security precautions upon installation.

  - Continue to install updates as they're made available by the people who wrote the blog software.

  - Deal with any security breaches that may occur.

Facebook

With Facebook you have two options: a profile account and a fan page. Facebook allows one profile account per person, and the person must use their real name and a valid email account. Facebook allows more than one fan page per person, and fan pages can be administered by logging into either a profile account or fan page account. If your fan page is for a business or organization and you want to add another administrator, add the person as an administrator by using their email address rather than selecting them from the fan list.

What you can do:

- Create profile account as detailed in Volume 1 of this series *Social Media for Beginners.*

- Create a Fan Page as detailed in Volume 4 of this series *Social Media Strategy.*

- Upload images and send status updates.

- Identify any added functionality you'd like in your profile account, such as a link or image for your badge (a badge is a small area Facebook gives you on your profile account to create your own content).

- Identify any added functionality you'd like on your fan page. This can be a wide range of options, almost as many options as you have for a website, but it requires a specific set of technical skills to add this functionality to your fan page.

How your designer can help:

• Design a custom image for your badge.

How your developer can help:

• You may want help editing or adding a video.

• You'll need a developer with experience in Facebook and FBML (a version of HTML specific to Facebook), as well as experience with PHP to customize your fan page beyond what it offers by default. For most people the default version is enough.

LinkedIn

What you can do:

• Create your LinkedIn account and begin to use as detailed in Volume 1 of this series *Social Media for Beginners*.

What your designer can do:

• There aren't ways at this time that a designer can help you.

What your web developer can do:

• Once you've exported your data from LinkedIn Contacts and saved your .csv file, you may want to import it into your CRM (customer relations management system) such as Outlook. You can try doing this yourself, though it may result in duplicate entries in your address book, or information getting into the wrong fields.

- Your web developer can help you remap the fields during import, or change the .csv file so it matches the way fields are set up in your CRM.

- Ask your web developer to write down the procedure they developed that resulted in a successful import while it's fresh in their mind, and ask for a copy of the procedure to keep with your files.

Twitter

What you can do:

- Create your Twitter account and begin to use as detailed in Volume 1 of this series *Social Media for Beginners*.

- Decide whether you want a custom background, and if so, how you want it to look.

How your designer can help:

- Create a custom background for you.

How your developer can help:

- Unless you want to create your own third-party Twitter application and you have lots of money to fund this, there isn't much of a role for your developer. You can handle most of what's possible on Twitter.

Online Issues

Security Issues

Because by nature a blog is a dynamic website, meaning it allows visitors to add their comments, it allows you and others you designate to log in and perform updates to the dynamic content, this means it has the potential to allow hackers with destructive intentions to find their way in and do some damage.

Are you and your developer prepared to deal with this added cost and responsibility along with gaining the extra flexibility in terms of look and functionality, or would you prefer to go the easier and less expensive route of a hosted blog?

I'm not saying that going with a hosted blog is any less risky in terms of getting hacked. I've talked with people who run these hosted blogs for a living and asked them about security breaches. Their answer, "It happens." I guess they just accept it as part of doing business online. It's up to you what you choose to risk.

Who Owns Your Content

Many websites that either serve or host your content would like very much to own the copyright to the material you post through their interface. The legalities of this haven't been ironed out, but if this is important to you it may be worthwhile to find the website's terms of service and have your legal people look it over before you post your valuable content.

If you run your own blog on your own server, this could minimize the possibility someone else might claim the rights to your copyrighted or personal material. On the other hand, if you then send the RSS feed of your blog to other websites (see Volume 4 of this series *Social Media Strategy*), then you're back posting on someone else's turf.

These and privacy issues are part of the new world we're creating with our online lives. The good news: The people using the services seem to have a say in what happens. In the social media world the users often point the direction in which the software application they're using will evolve. In the past when Facebook claimed they owned content posted by users, or began using user's photos alongside ads not related to the user, users rose up and complained loudly, and Facebook made adjustments.

We don't really know what all of this means yet. We trust Google to always 'do no harm', but as their servers and other search engines and websites continue to index so much information about us, we become more vulnerable. Or more protected. We don't really know what the future holds.

Summary

- Social media gives most of the power and control to you, the customer.

- You may want some help from a graphic designer or web developer to extend the default options of the social media tool you're using.

CHAPTER 5

Questions to Ask

ℭ

The Right Questions

Before knowing what to ask an Internet professional, you'll need to be very clear about what you want and need. Review your work from Volume 1 of this series *Social Media for Beginners* Chapter 2 "Quick Startup Checklist" and write a list of what you want. Leave a lot of room for notes by each item. This is a good time to use an Excel spreadsheet, so you can sort the list later by category.

Next look through Chapter 3 of this book "Designer or Developer" and put the name of the type of Internet professional you need for each item.

Then refer to Chapter 4 of this book "Social Media – Your Role and When to Get Help", and make notes next to each item regarding what you want to know or do that you hope your Internet professional will be able to handle for you.

Keep your worksheet handy as we go through the next section. You may want to start a separate Word or text document to take notes as well.

As you're becoming acquainted with an Internet professional and working on your first project, ask yourself these questions:

How comfortable are you with this person? What is your gut telling you? Your intellect may be right or wrong, but your gut usually has a valid point. If your gut is saying think twice, try to understand why. Is the Internet professional saying they can do something they really don't have the knowledge and experience to carry out? Or maybe you just always feel uncomfortable when you're in new territory. Does whatever you're feeling have any relationship to similar feelings you've had in the past, and how have those experiences turned out? How might you approach this time in a more effective manner?

Is this Internet professional listening to what you need, or forcing their solution without regard to what matters to you? Are they asking effective questions to get very clear about what you need?

Have they asked for your list of specs (or specifications)? If you don't have one, have they offered to help you create one? By the way, writing an accurate, detailed list of specifications can often be half the job of the entire project. Don't be surprised if they ask you to pay for this service.

Are they treating you with respect? How do they treat the people around them? Are they telling stories about how everyone in the past has taken advantage of them, or what's wrong with each of their former customers? Remember, at some point you may be one of those former customers. Do you want to be seen in this light?

How are they accustomed to handling the money? A reasonable way of handling this (with specific agreement in terms of the work to be accomplished) might be half or a third of the money up front, then the balance or second third upon delivery, and the last third a week later when the work has been tested and the bugs have been worked out. Be specific in terms of due dates. Some wonderful Internet professionals don't get in gear until they know when it's due.

Are they comfortable giving you references? When you contact those references, what can you learn about the integrity, dependability and skill of the Internet professional you're considering hiring? Did they deliver the project on time and to specifications? Were there any issues with money or other agreements? Did the person giving you the reference use any other Internet professionals, and did they have a positive experience? Do they have any advice for you as a customer?

Finding an Internet Professional

Where are they? How do you find a talented graphic designer or computer programmer you can trust, that you'll enjoy working with?

The first, most reliable source may be: Who do you know? Do you have a friend or colleague with a similar design or functionality on their website, blog or Twitter page that does what you want? If your friend will tell you who they worked with and give you honest information about their experience working with their vendor, this may be your best bet.

Alternatively, do you see a website or blog with elements of what you want? Look at the bottom of the home page to see if the designer or developer is listed. There may be a link to their home page, or if it's a templated site, a link to where you can find a similar template.

Next I go to my local schools where I've taken courses on Internet technology. I talk with the instructors, tell them what I'm looking for, and ask which students they'd recommend who are dependable and can produce quality work in this arena. Often you'll find very talented people who are willing to work for a bit less money to get their portfolio started, which is good for both of you.

Similarly, I look through the local paper to find user groups for the technology I'm interested in working with, and I show up at the meeting where I find many people with the necessary skills to do my job. I ask for business cards, do a little interviewing on the spot, and follow up later with the people I liked the most and ask for a demo.

I hear others talk about going to websites offering freelancers, and I've actually only heard positive stories. There must be some disappointments as well, but I haven't heard them. I don't have any experience with this personally.

I've heard mixed stories regarding outsourcing to other countries. Many of those developers are as talented or more so than developers here in the U.S., and accustomed to working for much less money. It can be more challenging to track a project, and I've heard some say the amount of time and effort it takes to communicate at that distance balances out to suggest it's just easier and more cost-effective to spend more money on local people you can work with face to face as needed. A few others show me their wonderful websites they paid very little money for, getting exactly what they wanted. So far I've opted to work with local people.

When you find some Internet professionals you trust, ask them who they work with (people they'd like to work with again). Your web developer probably already has a working relationship with a designer or two, and vice versa.

Do They Need a College Degree in Their Field?

In my experience a college degree is sometimes useful, and sometimes not relevant. For instance, the web developer I use was in one of the first graduating classes in computer technology, so he's grown up with the field as it has evolved. His school instilled him with deep knowledge of how to write code all the way from machine code to the finished product. His hair is a bit grey and he moves a bit slower, and he might tend toward older methods of writing functional code whereas a younger techie would feel more comfortable with object oriented programming, but he knows how the whole system works, he knows where something might break down, and he knows how to plan a web project so it'll be more flexible over time as needs change. He comments his code, and his code works. He's available to fix it should we find a bug.

I know other programmers who did not go to college, who studied their craft basically on their own, and who over time write very nice code. I also tried to work once with a graduate of an Ivy League school with a technology degree who probably knew a lot more than how to write a PHP script ... however what I needed was a PHP script that worked and his was the most inefficient set of scripts I've ever seen. And presumably because he's been to an Ivy League school in technology he wasn't at all interested in any of my PHP-related ideas. Though we finally gave up trying to work together, I will say we both tried.

So I say what's most important in this field is: Does the graphic look pleasing, and does it load quickly? Does the script work and load quickly, and does it have security built-in? And as important: Is it what you asked for? Ask to see samples of their previous work.

Getting Started

When I start working with someone new, I like to start with a small project that will give each of us an idea of how we'll work with each other. Here are some examples:

You: Choose a small project you won't stress over; something that's non-essential at the moment. If possible, schedule this so you'll have enough time to pay attention to clues you might pick as you work with this person. You can save so much time and money in the future if you take time to learn about and resolve potential issues now.

Social Media Specialist or **Strategist:** What is your top priority now? To pour out your heart and hopes to someone who can help you organize your dream into an overall strategy, or to just become effective in one small area of technology? Choose a topic you're already somewhat familiar with (you do know something now because you've been reading this book series!) so you can potentially gain some benefit by engaging this professional, but you'll also be able to gauge their level of expertise by referencing what you already know.

Graphic Designer: Going from smallest to largest as a first small project: badge for Facebook profile account, header for blog, or background for Twitter account.

Flash Designer: A first project might be a banner you can add to your website, or link to from your blog.

Flash Video: Unless you have several long, professional videos you want to stream on demand, YouTube might be a better solution for video these days. If you do have more video you want to stream from your website, you might give your Flash professional ten minutes of video or less and ask them to stream it for you as a Flash video. Review the section on page 36 and listen to see if they're using the same terminology and offering the same solutions. Also agree on a price before you both agree to the project. You may think it's a small project, but if they're charging by the hour and they're unfamiliar with the software, the money can add up fast.

Flash Developer: A first project might be a contact form in Flash, or perhaps the developer could give you a text file to update, that they in turn display in a small part of your website as your text scrolls through the Flash file they create. Ask for a scroll bar for visitors. Again, agree on a price before you begin the project. **Computer Programmer or Web Developer:** A contact form that saves submissions to a database could be a first place to start. Again, agree on a price before you begin the project.

System Administrator: Chances are this is a big project, so there may not be a way to test your working relationship with a small project. If you do anticipate huge amounts of traffic, a first project could be simply discussing the breadth of your overall project and what you anticipate in terms of traffic and file sizes. Are you planning a large sales push? Will this be a regular event or a one-time event? Have in hand data on your current website: file sizes, traffic, bandwidth, etc., and any server-related issues you've had.

Database Engineer: Any project with a database engineer is also probably a large project. Ask them what they know about normalizing databases and see if the term makes sense to them. If not, you may have a computer programmer and not a database engineer. This may be fine; it may be all you need. Normalizing a database means breaking down the data into several tables that relate to each other, so the same data is stored in only one place (and therefore only needs to be changed in one place) in your database. This is called first form, second form, third form and sometimes fourth form normalization.

Summary

First be very clear about what you want and need.

Determine which type of Internet professional can help you with each item:

> Social Media Specialist
> Graphic Designer
> Flash Designer
> Flash Video
> Flash Developer
> Computer Programmer or Web Developer
> System Administrator
> Database Engineer

Finding an Internet professional;

- Who do you know? Who do they know?

- Who created an online presence and design you like?

- Visit local schools

- Visit local user groups

- Referrals by other Internet professionals

- Websites offering freelancers

- Outsourcing

When you start working with someone new, start with a small project.

As you're working on your first project together, ask yourself:

- How comfortable are you with this person?

- Are they listening to what you need?

- Have they asked you for your list of specs, or for what you want?

- Are they treating you with respect?

- How are they accustomed to handling the money?

- What do their references say about having worked with them?

CHAPTER 6

Universal Needs Chart

ℰↄ

Why do I have this weird section about needs in a technical book about web development? Quite simply because I've found this concept can save a tremendous amount of time when dealing with people. Knowledge of how to communicate from a perspective of what each person needs can be especially helpful when working with technical people who are usually thinking more about what their computer program needs than what the people they're interacting with need. You be the catalyst to more effective conversation.

How it Works

Everyone has feelings and needs which propel them into behaviors, conclusions, choices and messages that may or may not be the best strategies to meet their needs. Most people are not conscious of which of their needs are driving them, or why they're so unhappy or unfulfilled.

Most people who react to the behaviors, conclusions, choices and messages of the people around them are also not aware of the person's needs, or their own needs as they react within their own habitual patterns.

We can spend countless hours, years and decades going around in circles explaining why it's someone else's fault, telling our same sad stories, railing against the same seemingly insurmountable conditions. The people around us can spend those same countless hours and decades debating the pros and cons with us, telling us why we shouldn't be so upset, arguing why they're not to blame and making their explanations.

Why doesn't this work? Because nobody has figured out what they really need. They're all arguing about strategies, having conflicts with what they perceive as 'the enemy'. The odd and amazing truth at the bottom of it all … we all have the same needs. Often people locked into the most difficult conflicts share exactly the same basic, universal needs. If they can get past their stories and enemy images and actually open their hearts to hear the human being they've locked horns with, chances are each party will discover they're both fighting for safety or recognition or significance or some other universal need. When they can both recognize this and drop the rest, it's also amazing how quickly they can agree on a strategy that will work for both of them.

What does this have to do with social media and time management?

I think it's useful to shortcut the chatter and drama and be able to identify, or at least make a heartfelt guess, as to the need someone we're dealing with might be trying to meet. Then hopefully instead of becoming embroiled in the hopeless mental landscape they've invited us into, we can come from a different place and have a more productive conversation for both of us.

It's also useful to be aware of our own needs so we can make our own choices based on meeting those needs. We'll be happier and healthier, and we'll spend much less time dithering and squander fewer resources on things that on the surface seem like they'll give us the safety, recognition or significance we're looking for, but actually just end up helping us feel a bit lonelier and more empty.

I include this list of needs because it's a useful reference when identifying the reason behind someone's behavior we don't understand, or our own feelings. When we can identify the need, we're very close to mediating conflicts, finding a solution that will work, or moving closer to a very fulfilling life.

How to Use the Chart

The following list of needs is neither exhaustive nor definitive. It is meant as a starting place to support anyone who wishes to engage in a process of deepening self-discovery and to facilitate greater understanding and connection between people.

For more information read *Conscious Networking* by Marilyn McLeod. For now, just use this list as a guide when trying to identify someone's underlying need to help you relate to them in a significant way.

Connection
acceptance
affection
appreciation
belonging
cooperation
communication
closeness
community
companionship
compassion
consideration
consistency
empathy
inclusion
intimacy
love

mutuality
nurturing
respect/self-respect
safety
security
stability
support
to know and be known
to see and be seen
to understand and
be understood
trust
warmth

Physical Wellbeing

air
food
movement/exercise
rest/sleep
sexual expression
safety
shelter
touch
water

Honesty

authenticity
integrity
presence

Play

joy
humor

Peace

beauty

communion
ease
equality
harmony
inspiration
order

Meaning

awareness
celebration of life
challenge
clarity
competence
consciousness
contribution
creativity
discovery
efficacy
effectiveness
growth
hope
learning
mourning
participation
purpose
self-expression
stimulation
to matter
understanding

Autonomy

choice
freedom
independence
space
spontaneity

CHAPTER 7

Follow Up

ॐ

I don't know how much of what you've just read you understand. Please be aware when I described technical things I was just skimming the surface. I wanted you to understand the general territory so you can speak more intelligently with techies you engage to help you with your social media and online marketing efforts.

If there is a particular aspect of your work that utilizes one specific piece of the puzzle, or one particular type of software, it may be worthwhile to study more in depth if that might help you define more clearly to your support people what you want, or perhaps deliver your portion (usually content or specifications) in a form that will save everyone time, and thus presumably save you money. The longer it takes for an Internet professional to understand what you want and translate what you give them into an end product, the more money they're likely to charge for their services. The more changes you ask them to make after the project is well on its way, the more time it will take them to complete the job.

Try to be as clear as possible in your agreements with the Internet professionals you hire to work with you. They should know exactly what the benchmarks are to receive how much money. You should know what to expect from them, and what they expect from you along the way. If you have someone who wants you to check their work incrementally, make time in your schedule to check in with them as they request. It'll save everyone time, money and frustration later.

Remember also, especially if you're someone who thrives on social connection, that many technical people are more comfortable communicating with other techies and with computers than with regular people. Not all techies are like that, but if you do meet an Internet professional who doesn't look you in the eye and who speaks in brief, monotone phrases, don't base your judgment of their ability to do the job on whether you think they like you or not, or whether you feel a warm, social connection from them. They may be very talented in creating exactly what you want even though they don't connect well socially. Look at their past work and talk to their references to see if they can deliver what you need.

Keep in mind, you're not going to know everything, no matter how much you study. No one can keep up with it all. When I get together with other social media people and we share what we know with each other, egos tend to be set aside and I hear things like, "Well, the link used to be here. If anyone knows where they moved it, please leave a message on my Fan Page discussion tab." We understand the general territory and we help each other find our way through the ever-changing landscape.

I hope I've left you with a better understanding of the online landscape, and I expect to see you here and there along our paths!

Join the conversation with me and watch for updates

http://www.Twitter.com/marilynmcleod
http://www.Facebook.com/7Steps
http://www.LinkedIn.com/in/coachmarilyn

Contact me!

I'd love to hear from you! Please let me know how this book is working for you, and check with the readers group with questions and to add new information you find!

My online hub: http://www.CoachMarilyn.com
My email: Marilyn@CoachMarilyn.com

Check http://www.CoachMarilyn.com for updated resources as social media and the Internet evolve and I learn more. Add what you've learned!

Marilyn McLeod
Marilyn@CoachMarilyn.com
San Diego 2010

www.ingramcontent.com/pod-product-compliance
Lightning Source LLC
Chambersburg PA
CBHW061026050326
40689CB00012B/2718